www.gardenpublishingco.com

The Heart of Worship

The Garden Training Center, Inc.
An Apostolic School of Ministry

Copyright ©2022 by The Garden Training Center, Inc.
Published by Garden Publishing Company LLC
For more information, please visit gardenpublishingco.com

All rights reserved. No parts of this publication may be reproduced, stored in a retrieval system, or transmitted in any form or by any means, electronic, mechanical, photocopying, recording, or otherwise, without the prior written permission of the copyright owner.

This book is sold subject to the condition that it shall not, by way of trade or otherwise, be lent, resold, hired out, or otherwise circulated without the publisher's prior consent in any form of binding or cover other than that in which it is published and without a similar condition including this condition being imposed on the subsequent purchaser. Under no circumstances may any part of this book be photocopied for resale.

Scripture taken from the New King James Version of the Bible ©. Used by Permission, all rights reserved.

ISBN 978-1-7355464-9-0
Cover design by Garden Publishing Co./BTSM
Interior design by Garden Publishing Co.

Printed in the United States of America.

Acknowledgments

Holy Spirit is the inspiration for the content of this book, however someone put words to it. This book was written by Grant Hill, Paula Green, and Jessica Doggett.

This book is one of a series of books written and distributed by The Apostolic School of Ministry from The Garden Training Center, Inc. The series arises from the foundational teachings of the school of ministry, founded by Brandy Helton. Brandy wrote several sections that are included in each book such as "God's Love" and the prayers included at the end of each book.

Many thanks to the team of writers of the series for their collaboration to make the series available to the public. The writers are: Lauren Caldwell, Jessica Doggett, Danetta Ferguson, Paula Green, Elisa Griffith, Nancy Hadley, Robin Harmon, Brandy Helton, Grant Hill, and Kevin McSpadden. Each have sought Holy Spirit for the words He wants to speak through them. The result is a mixture of personalities and communication strategies that convey the total message in a beautiful, diverse way.

A special thanks goes to Nancy Hadley, Kevin McSpadden and Chelsey Butcher with Garden Publishing Co., for their preparation and fine tuning of the text.

Encouragement and Prayer for the Reader

Beloved of God, these teachings are written to reveal Jesus Christ and His heart of love for all who call upon His name to save them.

God has sent His only begotten Son, Jesus Christ, to save all who would believe in Him and His Word.

God desires to reveal Himself and to give us His divine nature in Christ Jesus our Lord through the power of His Holy Spirit.

God is Jealous. He wants us to encounter His presence daily and walk with Him in glory – intimate communion - today, while it is called today, and forever.

It is my prayer that this teaching would so impact the readers that all would come to know and believe JESUS, the King of Kings and Lord of Lords, our Great God and Savior, and receive the PERFECT LOVE He has for us all as we grow up into Him and mature as true sons and daughters of God.

May you grow in faith and knowledge of your God and Savior and come to know the love that He has for you. I pray for you the Apostle Paul's prayer for spiritual growth:

Ephesians 3:14-21 The Living Bible (TLB)
"14-15 When I think of the wisdom and scope of his plan, I fall down on my knees and pray to the Father of all the great family of God—some of them already in heaven and some down here on earth— 16 that out of his glorious, unlimited resources he will give you the mighty inner strengthening of his Holy Spirit. 17 And I pray that Christ will be more and more at home in your hearts, living within you as you trust in him. May your roots go down deep into the soil of God's marvelous love; 18-19 and may you be able to feel and understand, as all God's children should, how long, how wide, how deep, and how high his love really is; and to experience this love for yourselves, though it is so great that you will never see the end of it or fully know or understand it. And so at last you will be filled up with God himself.
20 Now glory be to God, who by his mighty power at work within us is able to do far more than we would ever dare to ask or even dream of— infinitely beyond our highest prayers, desires, thoughts, or hopes. 21 May he be given glory forever and ever through endless ages because of his master plan of salvation for the Church through Jesus Christ."

In Christ our Lord,
Brandy Helton
A child of God

God's Love

God's love is good news! Don't believe the lie that God is distant, unapproachable, and angry!

God is love. He is the only true, eternal God. He is perfect and holy, and He is truth. God is One. He has revealed Himself in three distinct, individual, equal persons: God the Father, God the Son – Jesus, and God the Holy Spirit.

The Bible tells the story of God's perfect love. In that love, God created the first family to live on the earth with Him. Through their deep intimate relationship with the Father, Adam and Eve were meant to fulfill all that was in God's heart on Earth just like it is in Heaven, for God's glory and purposes. Adam and Eve were chosen to walk with God, clothed in His glory presence and were perfect, as He is perfect, and they lived in His beautiful garden, the secret place called Eden. He gave them His breath, life and power to have dominion over all He created and wanted them to reproduce that LIFE replenishing the earth with it, until all the earth is filled with His glory.

Genesis 1:26-28
"26 Then God said, 'Let Us make man in Our

image, according to Our likeness; let them have dominion over the fish of the sea, over the birds of the air, and over the cattle, over all the earth and over every creeping thing that creeps on the earth.' 27 So God created man in His own image; in the image of God He created him; male and female He created them. 28 Then God blessed them, and God said to them, 'Be fruitful and multiply; fill the earth and subdue it; have dominion over the fish of the sea, over the birds of the air, and over every living thing that moves on the earth.'"

God created His children in His likeness. He made them spirit beings, with a soul – mind, will and emotions – and placed them in a physical body. He gave His children the choice to love Him and to walk with Him in obedience to His every word. He gave the first family the power to overcome any temptation offered to them through God's adversary, the devil, who had rebelled against the Most High God in Heaven's glory and was cast down to the earth. The devil, Satan, brought great darkness and chaos prior to Adam and Eve's existence.

Adam and Eve were deceived into thinking that God was not perfect in love as Satan, the adversary, tempted them to believe that God would not keep His Word to them. Through their own will, Adam and Eve disobeyed the Father by eating from a tree that had the power to open their eyes to both good and evil. Through their choice of disobedience, they willfully gave their inheritance and authority over to the devil and his kingdom. Sin entered mankind, which produced death, eternal separation from a Holy God. Adam and Eve were banished from the dwelling and intimacy of perfection in the garden and were sent into the world as a fallen creation.

Father God knew He had to come Himself and save His family, and in His wisdom, He chose to send His Son, Jesus Christ into the world to save us and restore fallen mankind back to relationship with Him. Through His Son, He destroyed all the works of the devil and the curse of death. Hebrews 9:22 says, *"And according to the law almost all things are purified with blood, and without shedding of blood there is no remission."* Remission means to cancel the penalty, so according to the law there must be shedding of blood to cancel the penalty for sin. The Father cancelled the penalty for the sins of His children through the shedding of the blood of His innocent, holy Son Jesus, who was the Sent One, called and chosen to die for all, so all could live.

John 3:16-21

"16 For God so loved the world that He gave His only begotten Son, that whoever believes in Him should not perish but have everlasting life. 17 For God did not send His Son into the world to condemn the world, but that the world through Him might be saved. 18 'He who believes in Him is not condemned; but he who does not believe is condemned already, because he has not believed in the name of the only begotten Son of God. 19 And this is the condemnation, that the light has come into the world, and men loved darkness rather than light, because their deeds were evil. 20 For everyone practicing evil hates the light and does not come to the light, lest his deeds should be exposed. 21 But he who does the truth comes to the light, that his deeds may

be clearly seen, that they have been done in God.'"

Jesus was conceived by God's Holy Spirit in the womb of a young virgin named Mary. He appeared as the second Adam, in the flesh, with the choice to walk in perfect love and obedience, full of God's Spirit, as a man to do the will of His Father.

Jesus grew up as any male child did in the flesh but He had divine fellowship with His Father and Holy Spirit. At the appointed time, He was revealed as being sent from God to save. Jesus went around doing good and healed all who were oppressed by the devil spiritually and physically. He revealed His Father's heart and perfect love to all who believed through His teachings, grace and miraculous power.

Salvation means eternal life, healing, deliverance, protection, peace, wholeness, and forgiveness. Salvation came to all men through the cross, where the Son of God, the perfect One, was slaughtered as a lamb, bearing all sin for all times from a fallen people. Jesus bore the wrath of God against the darkness that separated God's family from Him. Jesus was punished for our sin and died to cleanse us from the guilt, shame and condemnation sin produces. Sin separates. Love restores.

Jesus was crucified, dead and buried, spending three days and nights in the depths of Hades, the realm of the dead fallen race. Jesus took back the keys of death and hell from that old serpent the devil, Satan, and therefore, all authority was restored back to Jesus.

Great Holy Spirit breathed LIFE into Jesus and raised Him from the dead. He appeared to His disciples, those who followed Him and obeyed His teachings. He showed them that He conquered sin, death and the grave and now, had the keys of hell and death, and would give ETERNAL LIFE to ALL who chose to believe in Him. King Jesus ascended back to the Father of glory where He ever lives to make intercession for us all, and He is coming again to the earth in power to establish His Father's Kingdom on Earth.

Jesus Christ is the head and Lord over His church, those who have made Him Lord and Savior, by believing He is the Son of the Living God and God in the flesh, who finished the work the Father gave Him to do. He not only died for our sins to save and heal us, He chose to give His authority to those He called and chose to follow Him as His disciples, His family.

Jesus has commissioned His followers to do the same works that He did while He lived on the earth.

John 14:12-14
"12 Most assuredly, I say to you, he who believes in Me, the works that I do he will do also; and greater works than these he will do, because I go to My Father. 13 And whatever you ask in My name, that I will do, that the Father may be glorified in the Son. 14 If you ask anything in My name, I will do it."

God loves us and desires that none should perish. He desires for His family to be with Him where He is. These books are written to inspire all who read them and to reveal the heart of God the Father, Jesus Christ the Son, and Holy Spirit in order that we might RECEIVE THE LOVE HE HAS FOR US and be CHANGED INTO HIS VERY LIKENESS. God desires to dwell with His family forever and ever just as He did in the beginning. How glorious it is to live in His presence and dominion, beholding His goodness, forever and ever, amen.

The book of Revelation describes the time that is coming when all things are made new according to God's heart of love:

Revelation 21:1-7
"1 Now I saw a new heaven and a new earth, for the first heaven and the first earth had passed away. Also, there was no more sea. 2 Then I, John, saw the holy city, New Jerusalem, coming down out of heaven from God, prepared as a bride adorned for her husband. 3 And I heard a loud voice from heaven saying, 'Behold, the tabernacle of God is with men, and He will dwell with them, and they shall be His people. God Himself will be with them and be their God. 4 And God will wipe away every tear from their eyes; there shall be no more death, nor sorrow, nor crying. There shall be no more pain, for the former things have passed away.' 5 Then He who sat on the throne said, 'Behold, I make all things new.' And He said to me, 'Write, for these words are true and faithful.' 6 And He said to me, 'It is done! I am the Alpha and the Omega, the Beginning and the End. I will give of the fountain of the water of life freely to him who thirsts. 7 He who overcomes shall inherit all things, and I will be his God and he shall be

My son.'"

To understand what is presented in the Bible, you must start by understanding God's love. The good news is that God loves you!

The Heart of It

To delve into the act of worshipping God, a believer in Christ Jesus must realize two important things: One, you were created by the Almighty God to behold Him, and two, you are the new temple, or dwelling, where the worship of this Almighty God takes place. The act of worship begins with this realization because the flesh resists true encounters with God, and the mind often resists the truth a believer was created to encounter - the holiness and glory of the all-powerful, perfect God of Heaven and Earth.

To know the heart of worship is to the know the heart of God. Throughout the Bible, God reveals Himself as a Father. He created a family for Himself, and He deeply desires this family to know Him: His ways, His thoughts, His actions, and even His kingdom. Jesus, who is the Son of God, revealed the Almighty as Father. Everything Jesus did, taught, or spoke was to open our eyes to the Father in Heaven. Therefore, as a man of God, everything Jesus did was unto to the Father as an act of worship to Him, giving us the example of what true worship looks like. True worship is to love the Lord your God with all your heart, soul, strength and mind in everything you do as a believer in Christ.

In the Body of Christ, we are told to gather together frequently, and not to neglect it, but instead continue to come together in remembrance of Christ, for teaching, prophesy and exhortation. These gatherings over time became known as times of "worship". They are not the only times a believer should worship, but instead be an addition to their personal, daily walk of encountering God in their bodily temple of worship. This book teaches about several facets of worship, both for the individual and within the corporate setting.

In this book are several sections explaining the various facets of the Father's heart that believers will encounter in worship. As you begin to know the heart of the Father, you inevitably want to worship Him more. The more you worship Him, the more of His heart you will encounter and the more of who He is you will behold. These "beholding encounters" take you to places in the heart of God as He chooses to reveal them. Each of these facets of worship are like "rooms" within the heart of God.

A previously published book explores worship in the throne room of God. This book will give the believer understanding in how to worship God in His healing presence, His divine romance, His prophetic, and in His quiet stillness. Ultimately, this book will take you deeper into the magnificent purpose of worship: to know and to glorify the heart of God.

The Heart of Worship

Chapter 1: Healing Presence of Worship

In our relationship with God, the intimacy of worship invites His presence into our lives in a such a way that our hearts receive tangible healing as peace and joy flood into our physical bodies. As we pause to worship Him, healing flows from the throne room of God in a spiritual outpouring that bursts forth into our physical world. Our faith in Jesus Christ and His finished work on the cross has brought us out of the darkness of the fallen world and into the marvelous light of His presence! Now Father God, our Creator, is ever before us, and when we acknowledge and yield to His presence, we can fully enjoy all the benefits of His glory. Through our repentance of sin and forgiveness through the blood of Jesus, we are made right with God and unashamedly enter His presence at any time. The Bible proclaims the blessing of our righteous status, which was granted through the sacrifice of Jesus.

Psalm 24:3-5
"3 Who may ascend into the hill of the Lord?
Or who may stand in His holy place?
4 He who has clean hands and a pure heart,

*Who has not lifted up his soul to an idol,
Nor sworn deceitfully.
5 He shall receive blessing from the Lord,
And righteousness from the God of his salvation."*

The Word reminds us that God works righteousness on our behalf. He alone has redeemed us from sin, death, and disease, and He has welcomed us into eternal life with Him. His abiding presence strengthens our inner man to live full and abundant lives to accomplish all the good things He has planned for us.

Psalm 103:3-5
*"3 He forgives all my sins
and heals all my diseases.
4 He redeems me from death
and crowns me with love and tender mercies.
5 He fills my life with good things.
My youth is renewed like the eagle's!"*

Furthermore, this healing presence is not just for the young, but the fullness of it is to be enjoyed even as we grow older.

Psalm 92:13-14
*"13 Those who are planted in the house of the Lord
Shall flourish in the courts of our God.
14 They shall still bear fruit in old age;
They shall be fresh and flourishing..."*

As children of God, we can seek Him in the presence of His holiness at any time, in any place, for encouragement, protection, and healing for our souls.

Psalm 63:1-8 (NLT)
"1 O God, you are my God; I earnestly search for you.
My soul thirsts for you; my whole body longs for you
in this parched and weary land where there is no water.
2 I have seen you in your sanctuary
and gazed upon your power and glory.
3 Your unfailing love is better than life itself;
how I praise you!
4 I will praise you as long as I live,
lifting up my hands to you in prayer.
5 You satisfy me more than the richest feast.
I will praise you with songs of joy.
6 I lie awake thinking of you,
meditating on you through the night.
7 Because you are my helper,
I sing for joy in the shadow of your wings.
8 I cling to you;
your strong right hand holds me securely."

When we encounter the love of God, we are forever changed! For many, these encounters occur during worship while we commune with Him through the Holy Spirit. Out of the overflow of His presence, there is healing and deliverance from the effects of this fallen world.

Several years ago, I encountered the Lord after weeks of praying and asking for healing from a lifetime of clinical depression. One day, as I was spending time in worship and enjoying His presence, I decided to lay down and immediately felt a peace flowing over me. I knew without a doubt that some kind of healing was taking place. Before I could even voice the question as to what was happening, I heard in my spirit, "It's the depression. IT'S GONE." Right at that moment, I felt something being lifted up and off of me. I was healed in that encounter, and I have been walking out my healing ever since.

In His presence, I found healing and the fullness of His Joy.

> **Psalm 16:11**
> *"11 You will show me the path of life;*
> *In Your presence is fullness of joy;*
> *At Your right hand are pleasures forevermore."*

The dwelling place of God, which is the "knowing" through faith that His healing presence is within and surrounding us, is key to living a healthier life. When we are communing with God, stress, fear, and darkness lift off of us. Not only is that good for our soul, but our bodies respond positively as well. As I began to spend more time in the awareness of His daily presence, I noticed I was feeling better overall and other recurring illnesses were no longer plaguing me as they had in the past. I happened upon this scripture one day and knew immediately why! His Word says it clearly, and not only can we claim these words over our lives, but we can walk them out by the Spirit of God.

> **Psalm 91:9-11**
> *"9 Because you have made the Lord, who is my refuge,*
> *Even the Most High, your dwelling place,*
> *10 No evil shall befall you,*
> *Nor shall any plague come near your dwelling;*

*11 For He shall give His angels charge over you,
To keep you in all your ways."*

The Angelic in the Presence of God

In the presence of God, surrounding His throne are angels created to worship Him. In the Old Testament scripture, the prophet Isaiah recorded his experience in the temple of the Lord before the altar of His Presence. Here Isaiah described this amazing scene in great detail:

Isaiah 6:1-3
*"1 In the year that King Uzziah died, I saw the Lord sitting on a throne, high and lifted up, and the train of His robe filled the temple. 2 Above it stood seraphim; each one had six wings: with two he covered his face, with two he covered his feet, and with two he flew. 3 And one cried to another and said:
"Holy, holy, holy is the Lord of hosts;
The whole earth is full of His glory!"*

God granted Isaiah to witness the majesty and glory of worship in His very throne room. As Isaiah saw, mighty and beautiful angels engaged in heartfelt worship, proclaiming God's holiness and glory. In the holy presence of God, Isaiah was immediately aware of his fallen nature as everything was laid bare:

Isaiah 6:5-7
*"5 "Woe is me, for I am undone!
Because I am a man of unclean lips,
And I dwell in the midst of a people of unclean lips;
For my eyes have seen the King,*

The Lord of hosts."
6 Then one of the seraphim flew to me, having in his hand a live coal which he had taken with the tongs from the altar. 7 And he touched my mouth with it, and said:
"Behold, this has touched your lips;
Your iniquity is taken away,
And your sin purged."

Notice that the angel served the believer in the atmosphere of worship. While worship permeated the entire room, Isaiah repented from his heart, and the angel came to cleanse him with a live coal from the altar. This cleansing applies to us as well. As repentant and redeemed believers in the Lord Jesus Christ, He has cleansed us from all unrighteousness through His blood.

While the above passage highlights how angels minister to God's people during worship, the Lord also sends His Word to heal us. One important job of angels is to heed God's word and carry it out to fulfill His desires.

Psalm 107:19-20
"19 Then they cried out to the Lord in their trouble,
And He saved them out of their distresses.
20 He sent His word and healed them,
And delivered them from their destructions."

Psalm 103:20-21
"20 Bless the Lord, you His angels,
Who excel in strength, who do His word,
Heeding the voice of His word.
21 Bless the Lord, all you His hosts,
You ministers of His, who do His pleasure.

In addition to their ministry of cleansing and healing, God has given angels the assignment to help believers in times of need."

Hebrews 1:14
"14 Are they not all ministering spirits sent forth to minister for those who will inherit salvation?"

Finally, angels also watch over and protect believers from harm and evil. The early church body found help from angels during persecution as they were locked up in prison for vocalizing their faith in Jesus Christ, performing healings and miracles in His Name. The book of Acts is filled with accounts of the believing church in a lifestyle of worship, prayer, and a continual yielding to the presence of God and the infilling of the Holy Spirit. I believe this was key to the accounts where angels would come to free them while in chains and instruct them to carry on with their words of life.

Acts 5:19
"19 But at night an angel of the Lord opened the prison doors and brought them out..."

Acts 12:5-10
"5 Peter was therefore kept in prison, but constant prayer was offered to God for him by the church. 6 And when Herod was about to bring him out, that night Peter was sleeping, bound with two chains between two soldiers; and the guards before the door were keeping the prison. 7 Now behold, an angel of the Lord stood by him, and a light shone in the prison; and he struck Peter on the side and raised him up, saying, "Arise quickly!" And his chains fell off his hands. 8 Then the angel said to him, "Gird

yourself and tie on your sandals"; and so he did. And he said to him, "Put on your garment and follow me." 9 So he went out and followed him, and did not know that what was done by the angel was real, but thought he was seeing a vision. 10 When they were past the first and the second guard posts, they came to the iron gate that leads to the city, which opened to them of its own accord; and they went out and went down one street, and immediately the angel departed from him."

Worship launches angels into their God-given assignment of ministering to His people. Angels, in their variety of ministries, love to join in magnifying the Lord alongside the people of God. While we must never allow the angels themselves to become the focus, we can expect to experience the ministry of these majestic and powerful beings as we worship the One Who created both us and them. It is a glorious co-laboring that empowers us to glorify God, which, as we have noted several times, is our highest calling.

God's Presence is Our Calling

As believers, we are called to take God's healing presence to others as a sign to them that Jesus is Lord! When we speak the truth about the good news of the Kingdom of God, He will back up His word with signs, miracles, and healings. Because of the Holy Spirit within us and His presence upon us, the unbeliever in our midst can experience the undeniable love that Jesus offers through us.

Mark 16:15-20 (NLT)
"15 And then He (Jesus) told them, "Go into all

the world and preach the Good News to everyone. 16 Anyone who believes and is baptized will be saved. But anyone who refuses to believe will be condemned. 17 These miraculous signs will accompany those who believe: They will cast out demons in my name, and they will speak in new languages. 18 They will be able to handle snakes with safety, and if they drink anything poisonous, it won't hurt them. They will be able to place their hands on the sick, and they will be healed."

19 When the Lord Jesus had finished talking with them, he was taken up into heaven and sat down in the place of honor at God's right hand. 20 And the disciples went everywhere and preached, and the Lord worked through them, confirming what they said by many miraculous signs. (Emphasis added)"

As we go about our daily lives, we must encourage ourselves and one another in these words and believe them by faith. The presence of God was so tangible with the apostle Peter that people in the path of his shadow were healed.

Acts 5:14-16
"14 And believers were increasingly added to the Lord, multitudes of both men and women, 15 so that they brought the sick out into the streets and laid them on beds and couches, that at least the shadow of Peter passing by might fall on some of them. 16 Also a multitude gathered from the surrounding cities to Jerusalem, bringing sick people and those who were tormented by unclean spirits, and they were all healed."

We can remind ourselves of Peter as we walk through the corridors of a hospital, knowing that the presence of our God, the Healer, is with us.
The presence of God in our lives is so palpable that even our clothing can be anointed for healing, as we see in the example of the apostle Paul.

Acts 19:11-12
"11 Now God worked unusual miracles by the hands of Paul, 12 so that even handkerchiefs or aprons were brought from his body to the sick, and the diseases left them and the evil spirits went out of them."

At this point you may be thinking, "Well I'm just an ordinary person, certainly not an apostle." Nevertheless, the truth is you also have been specifically called, strategically placed, and spiritually trained to go and do the same! Remember that even if you don't feel you have the head knowledge, you do have the Holy Spirit, and 1 John 2:27 says that He will teach you all you need for the tasks to which He calls you. Hopefully, you are also connected with the government of God in proper authority, since that will empower you for ministry.

Ephesians 4:11-12
"11 And He Himself gave some to be apostles, some prophets, some evangelists, and some pastors and teachers, 12 for the equipping of the saints for the work of ministry, for the edifying of the body of Christ."

As you can see, Jesus establishes certain offices for the explicit purpose of equipping believers to carry out the work of the Kingdom. This divine arrangement also works to ensure that these same saints (believers within the church body) may call upon their leaders when they find themselves in need of healing.

James 5:14-16
"14 Is anyone among you sick? Let him call for the elders of the church, and let them pray over him, anointing him with oil in the name of the Lord. 15 And the prayer of faith will save the sick, and the Lord will raise him up. And if he has committed sins, he will be forgiven. 16 Confess your trespasses to one another, and pray for one another, that you may be healed. The effective, fervent prayer of a righteous man avails much."

What a beautiful depiction of the Body of Christ operating under the healing power of the presence of God! As you worship the everlasting God, you come to fully embrace His healing presence within and around you. May you be encouraged and strengthened in your faith as healing is manifested to you and all those you shall encounter.

I want to share a song that was birthed during an encounter I had with the Lord in the beauty of His Holiness. Truly, He is the Lord Who Heals us, catching every single tear, redeeming all the broken places within our hearts as we yield to His love.

There is a place that few will go, come with me, come with me.
Come with me in His majesty, come with me, come with me.

The shame that you're holding so dear to your heart, the anger that tries to consume.
The pain in your body that keeps you from life my Jesus has these words for you.
"I died for that! I set you free....the moment I saw you, with Me."
Oh yes, I died for that, I took your fears, the moment I saw....your tears.
There is a place that few will go, come with me, come with me.
Come with me in His majesty, come with me, come with me.
The death of a dream so fresh in your mind, the people you thought that you knew.
The life that you had.... that all slipped away, my Jesus has these words for you.
"I died for that! I set you free....the moment I saw you, with Me."
Oh yes, I died for that, I took your fears, the moment I saw....your tears.
And I will never stop telling you, never stop telling you.... I love you; I love you child.

The love of God as a Father to a child is not the only way we encounter the love of God in worship. We can also encounter the love of God as the Bridegroom and the believers, the church, as His bride.

Chapter 2: Divine Worship – The Bride of Jesus

To give reverence and honor to God opens our spirit, soul, and body to encounter the divinity of God. The worship of God is divine because it is a supernatural occurrence! Think about it: worship involves flesh and bone beings (humans) entering the pure and holy presence of the Creator of the universe. That is impossible without supernatural empowerment. However, the fact that worship is supernatural doesn't mean it is complicated. As a believer, I never set out to worship God; I just fell in love with Him, and out of that relationship, worship was birthed.

So how can we, that are made of flesh, worship a God Who is spirit? As we do with everything that pertains to God, it is by faith.

Hebrews 11:6
"6 But without faith it is impossible to please Him, for he who comes to God must believe that He is, and that He is a rewarder of those who diligently seek Him.
Practically speaking, we begin worship by acknowledging God's presence with praise and thanksgiving!"

Psalm 100:4
"4 Enter into His gates with thanksgiving,
And into His courts with praise.
Be thankful to Him, and bless His name."

This praise and worship of our divine God is not

only about the songs we sing in a church setting, but is actually intended to be a lifestyle of ministering our love to Him and allowing Him to love us. We may start with shouts of joy and as His presence becomes more clear to us. On the other hand, we may find ourselves settling back or even lying down as we encounter what feels like a thick, weighty presence. This is often referred to as the weight of His Glory! Here are just two scriptures that testify to the reality of His divine presence:

2 Chronicles 5:13-14
"13 indeed it came to pass, when the trumpeters and singers were as one, to make one sound to be heard in praising and thanking the Lord, and when they lifted up their voice with the trumpets and cymbals and instruments of music, and praised the Lord, saying:
"For He is good,
For His mercy endures forever,"
that the house, the house of the Lord, was filled with a cloud, 14 so that the priests could not continue ministering because of the cloud; for the glory of the Lord filled the house of God."

1 Kings 8:10-11 (ESV)
"10 And when the priests came out of the Holy Place, a cloud filled the house of the Lord, 11 so that the priests could not stand to minister because of the cloud, for the glory of the Lord filled the house of the Lord."

However we may experience it, worship was always intended by God to be an intimate act, especially as we grow in our relationship with Him. Intimacy in its simplest form is defined as a close, familiar, and usually affectionate or loving personal relationship with another person or group (dictionary.com). Intimate relationships include detailed knowledge of or deep understanding of the other person(s). If you look closely enough, even the word itself hints at its deeper meaning – "IN TO ME SEE". Intimacy is a crucial part of life because everyone longs to be accepted in the deepest, most inmost place of our being. The good news is that the One Who created us, the God of the universe, already knows the secret place of our heart, and longs for us to willingly open it up to Him.

Psalm 139:1-4
"1 O Lord, You have searched me and known me.
2 You know my sitting down and my rising up; You understand my thought afar off.
3 You comprehend my path and my lying down, And are acquainted with all my ways.
4 For there is not a word on my tongue, But behold, O Lord, You know it altogether."

Another translation renders Psalm 139:3 as saying, "*You are so intimately aware of me, Lord. You read my heart like an open book*". (TPT)

The Psalmist, King David, understood this cry of "IN TO ME SEE, LORD" and continues in his prayer to God:

Psalm 139:23-24
"23 Search me, O God, and know my heart; Try me, and know my anxieties;
24 And see if there is any wicked way in me, And lead me in the way everlasting."

The above excerpts from the Psalms were written as a song unto the Lord. Divine worship quite frequently includes songs, as music can reach depths in our soul and unlock passions that flow forth in the presence of God in response to His love for us. As with many parts of our walk with the Lord, worship through song is a response to the love God pours out on us.

1 John 4:19
"19 We love Him because He first loved us."

Not only does God love us perfectly, but He has also given us the Holy Spirit to constantly reveal His love. It is within the context of love that we truly understand the covenant God has made with us to love us forever. Jesus is the fulfillment of that covenant, and one of the Holy Spirit's most important jobs is to draw us through love to Jesus Christ our Lord and Bridegroom.

Isaiah 54:5a
*"5 For your Maker is your husband,
The Lord of hosts is His name..."*

2 Corinthians 11:2
"2 For I am jealous for you with godly jealousy. For I have betrothed you to one husband, that I may present you as a chaste virgin to Christ."

When Christ returns for us, His covenant bride, consuming love will bring us to our final home with Him as we celebrate with a feast!

John 14:3
"3 And if I go and prepare a place for you, I

will come again and receive you to Myself; that where I am, there you may be also."

Song of Solomon 2:4
"4 He brought me to the banqueting house, And his banner over me was love."

Revelation 19:7-9
7 Let us be glad and rejoice and give Him glory, for the marriage of the Lamb has come, and His wife has made herself ready." 8 And to her it was granted to be arrayed in fine linen, clean and bright, for the fine linen is the righteous acts of the saints. 9 Then he said to me, "Write: 'Blessed are those who are called to the marriage supper of the Lamb!' " And he said to me, "These are the true sayings of God."

As we wait in joyful hope for the coming of our Bridegroom King Jesus, we have the opportunity and privilege of worshipping Him now through the Holy Spirt, who bears witness with us of His coming:

Revelation 22:17
"17 And the Spirit and the bride say, "Come!" And let him who hears say, "Come!" And let him who thirsts come. Whoever desires, let him take the water of life freely."

The Word of God has historically testified of this love story and will continue to do so throughout all eternity. Jesus beckons us to cling to Him in this intimate relationship through divine worship. Just as fruit is only produced through the vine, our lives are only richly productive as we depend upon Him.

John 15:4
"4 Abide in Me, and I in you. As the branch cannot bear fruit of itself, unless it abides in the vine, neither can you, unless you abide in Me."

This intimate lifestyle of abiding in Him is our love story. To abide with Jesus means to believe fully in Him, to obey Him, to trust Him, and to interact with Him on a moment-by-moment basis. The Song of Solomon tells of a loving romance between a man and a woman, but for those with spiritual ears to hear and eyes to see, it is the story of Jesus the bridegroom and us, the bride! First, we both acknowledge that we each belong to the other:

Song of Solomon 2:16a
"16 My beloved is mine, and I am his."

Song of Solomon 6:3a
"3 I am my beloved's, And my beloved is mine."

As a result of this intimate union, Jesus calls us to Himself, to come away with Him:

Song of Solomon 2:13b
"13 Rise up, my love, my fair one, And come away!"

As lovers of Christ Jesus, His Bride, our response can be just as intimate as we run after Him.

Song of Solomon 1:4
"4 Draw me away! We will run after you..."

We belong to our beloved and He gives Himself to

us. He calls and we respond. He draws, we pursue. This intimacy, this romance with our Lord, produces fruit beyond measure in our lives. Without it, Jesus taught that we do not bear fruit. That's why it is important to make worship a priority.

Although it is wonderful and a good discipline to make special times to spend in worship, it does not always have to be the perfect setting. In fact, it is often during our most difficult times that divine worship of our bridegroom Jesus will bring us the most peace. He also performs miracles in the midst of our worship, like those we witness in the Word with these followers of Jesus who had been thrown into prison for their faith.

Acts 16:25-26
"25 But at midnight Paul and Silas were praying and singing hymns to God, and the prisoners were listening to them. 26 Suddenly there was a great earthquake, so that the foundations of the prison were shaken; and immediately all the doors were opened and everyone's chains were loosed."

Jesus will meet us in the midst of anything. One woman found herself desperate to worship Jesus in the middle of a dinner party. She dropped to her knees, positioned herself behind Him, and let her tears fall to wash His feet before she wiped them with her hair. Luke describes the event as follows:

Luke 7:36-38
"36 Then one of the Pharisees asked Him to eat with him. And He went to the Pharisee's house, and sat down to eat. 37 And behold, a woman in

> *the city who was a sinner, when she knew that Jesus sat at the table in the Pharisee's house, brought an alabaster flask of fragrant oil, 38 and stood at His feet behind Him weeping; and she began to wash His feet with her tears, and wiped them with the hair of her head; and she kissed His feet and anointed them with the fragrant oil."*

What honor this bold woman received, to wash the feet of her King and anoint His head with oil! The others present sat at the table with Jesus, but she kissed His feet. They were nearby, but she touched the Living Word of God, ministering to Him in this intimate moment. Like the woman described in that passage, the opportunity for intimate worship is ever before us, no matter our current circumstances. We can "step in" to His presence by faith simply by acknowledging that He is there as we open our hearts to the Bridegroom King, Jesus.

Revelation 3:20
> *"20 Behold, I stand at the door and knock. If anyone hears My voice and opens the door, I will come in to him and dine with him, and he with Me."*

The Love of God will continually draw the believer into the place where your heart rejoices with "IN TO ME SEE, LORD!" Your fellowship with the Father, the Son, and the Holy Spirit will fill you with the voice of God. When we hear the voice of God, He asks the believer to act. These actions in worship lead us into our next section, worshiping God in His prophetic anointing.

Chapter 3: Prophetic Worship

The next facet of worship is one that invites a believer to co-labor with God. Prophetic worship engages a believer to act, to declare, to dance, to sing, or even pluck and play an instrument, all according to the orchestration of the Holy Spirit during a time of worship. In 1 Corinthians we read we are co-laborers with Christ:

1 Corinthians 3:9
9 "For we are God's fellow workers; you are God's field, you are God's building."

The act of worship most often consists of believers offering themselves (body, soul and spirit) in adoration of the Almighty God. We have also seen how worship is intimate in His Divine Presence and even peaceful as we learn to rest in Him. Prophetic worship occurs when Holy Spirit empowers you to reveal what is happening spiritually through a physical action. Under His leadership, you become a fellow participant in the worship of Heaven. The actions Holy Spirit directs in worship reveal God's heart, God's purposes, and God's ways through music, song, dance or declaration.

Prophetic worship is very simple when you can define the term "prophetic." The prophetic is simply perceiving the heart and thoughts of God and then releasing them individually or corporately. How can you perceive the heart of God? You worship Him in His Divine Presence. Christ wants to know His children. He calls His church

His "Bride," and believers pursue Him as a bride waiting in the night for her bridegroom to come. In this intimate place, Holy Spirit will speak and bring encounters to a worshipper of God. Scripture declares that the Spirit of God knows God's heart and reveals it to believers.

> **1 Corinthians 2:10-11**
> *"10 But God has revealed them to us through His Spirit. For the Spirit searches all things, yes, the deep things of God. 11 For what man knows the things of a man except the spirit of the man which is in him? Even so no one knows the things of God except the Spirit of God."*

When a believer hears, sees, or encounters the Holy Spirit during worship, sometimes God will lead that individual to reveal this encounter to another. The purpose of such prophetic worship is to demonstrate God's heart and thoughts upon the earth. Throughout the Bible, the prophetic makes known God's thoughts, intentions, and emotions of His heart to His children and the people of the earth. In the same way, prophetic worship reveals God's thoughts, intentions and emotions of His heart through acts of worship, usually via song, music, and dance.

When a believer perceives the intentions of Holy Spirit during worship, prophetic worship will reveal it individually or corporately. For example, sometimes a song needs to be sung specifically for an individual; sometimes a dance needs to be displayed publicly for an entire corporate body of believers. Each is powerful and purposeful in its own way, and each represents one way we co-labor with God in prophetic worship.

Prophetic worship, then, is the fruit of the divine romance of worship. It is when you perceive the heart of God and sing, speak, play musically God's intentions to an individual or to a corporate body.

Three Mediums of Prophetic Worship

In general, there are three main mediums, or channels, through which a believer engages in worship. The first is by speaking to God or declaring who God is in praise and thanksgiving. The second is through singing from the heart. The third is an act of giving praise and worship to God through music, instrumentation, or even dance. Each of the mediums of worship brings a beauty, a rhythm, and even an order to how a body of believers encounters God. Each of these three channels of worship can be used by God prophetically to reveal His ways. Let's look at some examples in scripture:

Speaking and Declaring God's Word in Prophetic Worship:

> **Nehemiah 9:3**
> *"3 And they stood up in their place and read from the Book of the Law of the Lord their God for one-fourth of the day; and for another fourth they confessed and worshiped the Lord their God."*

Here Nehemiah and Ezra gather the children of Israel to worship God and as they were worshipping, the people confessed, or spoke, before God. This is a very similar picture to what occurs in Christian churches every Sunday. Prophetic worship sees the people declare God's prophesies during worship. Let's read an account in **2 Chronicles 5:13-6:2**:

> *"13 indeed it came to pass, when the trumpeters and singers were as one, to make one sound to be heard in praising and thanking the Lord, and when they lifted up their voice with the trumpets and cymbals and instruments of music, and praised the Lord, saying:*
> *"For He is good,*
> *For His mercy endures forever,"*
> *that the house, the house of the Lord, was filled with a cloud, 14 so that the priests could not continue ministering because of the cloud; for the glory of the Lord filled the house of God.*
>
> *6:1 Then Solomon spoke:*
> *"The Lord said He would dwell in the dark cloud.*
> *2 I have surely built You an exalted house,*
> *And a place for You to dwell in forever."*

In this account, we see that a worship service had congregated with King Solomon and the priests. Indeed, this was a very special service as it was first time in history the Ark of the Covenant was placed in a permanent temple. The priests lead the congregation of Israel in worship with music and singing, "The Lord is good and endures forever." The Holy Spirit then revealed himself as cloud, but then King Solomon spoke. In the midst of the glorious scene, God moved upon the heart of King Solomon to declare and prophesy that this temple was a place for God to dwell in forever. This description is a great example of how a believer may speak a prophecy within the midst of worship. The Bible has many more examples of such prophecy arising from the heart of worship:

Psalm 71:17
"17 O God, You have taught me from my youth; And to this day I declare Your wondrous works."

Psalm 75:9
"9 But I will declare forever, I will sing praises to the God of Jacob."

Psalm 96:1-3
"1 Oh, sing to the Lord a new song! Sing to the Lord, all the earth. 2 Sing to the Lord, bless His name; Proclaim the good news of His salvation from day to day. 3 Declare His glory among the nations, His wonders among all peoples."

Psalm 102:21
"21 To declare the name of the Lord in Zion, And His praise in Jerusalem..."

You may have noticed there are two things in common with the verses above: they are each from Psalms and they each instruct the reader to "declare" while giving worship and praise unto God. The fact that these are scriptures within Psalms reveal they themselves were musically crafted. Psalms were poetic songs or spoken words given during worship over the accompaniment of music! Many Psalms are in their entirety a prophesy of the coming Messiah Jesus. (For examples of prophetic psalms, read Psalm 22, Psalm 45 and Psalm 2.) The book of Psalms reveals the nature of speaking and declaring God's prophesies during music. Furthermore, the Psalms show that worship is a desire of God's heart for His people to practice to this day. Notice in Colossians:

Colossians 3:16
"16 Let the word of Christ dwell in you richly in all wisdom, teaching and admonishing one another in psalms and hymns and spiritual songs, singing with grace in your hearts to the Lord."

Christians are told to practice teaching and admonishing each other when gathered by speaking the Psalms in worship to declare God's faithfulness and reveal His glory to one another. This verse also leads us to our next medium of prophetic worship, singing.

Singing in Prophetic Worship

Singing prophetically actually occurs quite a bit within the Bible. One of the first instances is the book of Numbers:

Numbers 21:16-17
"16 From there they went to Beer, which is the well where the Lord said to Moses, "Gather the people together, and I will give them water." 17 Then Israel sang this song:
"Spring up, O well!
All of you sing to it—"

The Israelites have become thirsty in their wilderness journey and the Lord tells Moses to gather them together, for "I will give them water." God reveals His intentions and His heart to Moses in this instance, which is an example of the prophetic. Instead of Moses prophesying through the spoken word, the people of Israel engage themselves in agreement with God's heart to give them water by singing prophetically to the well of water to spring forth! The people prophesied through singing that the well would spring up and produce a stream of water for them.

As with other mediums of prophetic worship, the Bible has many examples of prophetic singing:

Psalm 98:1-2
"1 Oh, sing to the Lord a new song!
For He has done marvelous things;
His right hand and His holy arm have gained Him the victory.
2 The Lord has made known His salvation;
His righteousness He has revealed in the sight of the nations."

Ephesians 5:19
"19 speaking to yourselves in psalms and hymns and spiritual songs, singing and making melody in your hearts to the Lord."

These are just two of the verses written as encouragement for a believer to sing to the Lord a new song. In Ephesians the believers are instructed to sing to each other in psalms hymns and spiritual songs. These new songs were to be inspired and led by the encounters with Holy Spirit. As you encounter God's goodness and glory in worship, sing to Him a new song. As you gather together and hear God's voice, reveal His desires to each other with spiritual songs and hymns.

What does each of these mean practically? As we've mentioned, Psalms were poetic songs, sometimes spoken, sometimes sung, by the people of God to declare God's praise, purposes, and sovereignty. Hymns are vocal arrangements of melodies for congregations to give worship and praise to God. Spiritual songs are musical arrangements, melodic singing, or prophetic spiritual songs revealing the heart of God by the Holy Spirit as only the Spirit can do. In the Old Testament we see instances where the prophets would actually arrange their prophecies to music either be sung or declared in the rhythm of the music (See Habakkuk 3:1,19). These are examples of prophetic worship through the medium of singing.

Music and Instruments in Prophetic Worship

So far, we've made it clear that speaking and singing are both channels, or mediums, of prophecy that spring forth out of the believer's encounter with God in worship. However, sometimes, God chooses to speak through His people even when no words are spoken or sung. This takes place through the music and/or instruments as believers submit to the orchestration of the Holy Spirit.

God created all of creation to praise His name. Throughout scripture we read about a cry for all creation to give glory to God. In Isaiah, we read a joyful prophesy about the trees of the field clapping their hands while the mountains break forth in singing (Isaiah 55). Creation has a spiritual "voice" to worship God with, and mankind has created musical instruments with various elements of creation. Each of these instrument groups can be used by believers to praise God and can therefore be used to prophetically worship with God as well.

Every instrument in music brings a unique sound, or variation of sounds, to usher in beauty and vibrancy to music. These sounds minister to heart and soul of a man. In 1 Samuel we see that David's playing of the harp soothed King Saul's soul when he was distressed:

1 Samuel 16:23
"23 And so it was, whenever the spirit from God was upon Saul, that David would take a harp and play it with his hand. Then Saul would become refreshed and well, and the distressing spirit would depart from him."

The sound of the harp's melodic notes soothed Saul and brought him freedom from an evil spirit. In the same way, music and instruments can bring God's voice, emotions, intentions, and encounters to individuals and congregations prophetically. At the end of Psalms, God tells us to use every instrument group to praise His name:

Psalm 150:3-5
*"3 Praise Him with the sound of the trumpet;
Praise Him with the lute and harp!
4 Praise Him with the timbrel and dance;
Praise Him with stringed instruments and flutes!
5 Praise Him with loud cymbals;
Praise Him with clashing cymbals!"*

Each modern instrument group is mentioned in these three verses: strings, brass, woodwinds, and percussion. Each of these instrument groups are unique and used differently within an orchestra or band arrangement. Brass instruments shout and proclaim! Woodwinds provide joyous melodies. Percussion instruments bring rhythm and timing to whole piece. Finally, the string instruments provide the body, emotions, and depth to the sounds of creation. Because of this, in Ephesians believers are told to "pluck", or make melodies, within your heart towards God and your brothers and sisters in Christ. This action of plucking your heart strings is a comparison to playing a harp - you are to pluck and prophetically worship God from the depths of your heart, just like the depth of emotion that can be played from the notes of a harp.

God may even use a prophetic sound to move in supernatural ways. Recall the story of the fall of Jericho:

Joshua 6:20
"20 So the people shouted when the priests blew the trumpets. And it happened when the people heard the sound of the trumpet, and the people shouted with a great shout, that the wall fell down flat. Then the people went up into the city, every man straight before him, and they took the city."

At God's direction, the priests blew trumpets, then the people yelled with all their might, and the wall of Jericho fell down, allowing the city to be breached. Yet notice in the natural this event could not have occurred - it was impossible. Prophetically, the trumpets were proclaiming that these "impenetrable" walls were going to fall down. When the people were shouting the walls were going to fall down, that was co-laboring with God's intentions and prophetically engaging in them. Then by the supernatural, the walls of Jericho crumbled in their sight. This is what prophetic worship is all about: bringing forth God's intentions through instruments and voices praising and worshipping God until it comes forth!

The Arts and Prophetic Worship

These three mediums are just the main channels used in worship, but there are many art forms to worship God and prophetically worship Him. Some believers paint prophetically as the Holy Spirit shows them what to paint. Many worshipers dance; indeed, in Psalm 150 we read believers are to praise Him with the dance. Whichever artful way we worship God, the Holy Spirit can use it prophetically. Sculptures, plays, books, videography, photography, flags and décor all can be produced for the glory of God, and with each art form God can use it to prophesy His heart, until all the earth knows the glory of God.

Prophetic worship engages a believer to take action before God and release His intentions through the worship of singing, declaring, the arts and musicianship. Whichever facet of worship a believer engages, the focus is always on encountering, and in some cases, revealing, the heart of the One we worship. Yet even in the stillness of God a believer is called to know Him. Worship is not always action, yet another facet of worship is learning how to be still and listen.

Chapter 4: Worshipping in the Quiet Place

Resting in the Lord's presence is vital in being made into the image of Christ. How can you transform into the likeness of someone you do not even know? It's impossible. In order to allow the Holy Spirit to carry out His work of making us like Jesus, we must spend time in His presence, gazing upon His beauty and giving Him the reverence He is due.

As an illustration of the necessity of resting in worshiping God, think about how pickles are made. Pickles have to sit in the jar with all the seasonings and juices for a while before they're fully saturated. Once they remain in the jar long enough, pickles take on all the flavors they've soaked in all that time. Our experience in worship can be very similar.

In spiritual terms, being with Jesus in a quiet place has to do with immersing yourself, being saturated in His presence, or in His Word. It's here that you're getting to know Him intimately, which helps you reflect His ways and His character. This truth is the whole heart of John 15. I like call this the abiding chapter. To abide with Jesus, and Him alone, is of the utmost importance to your walk with Him. Jesus Himself made it clear that we can bear no fruit apart from Him. Abiding in His presence is what shapes and molds us into who we are called to be in Christ. This time with Jesus is irreplaceable. It is in this intimate communion that we learn to surrender and allow Him to move, lift burdens, speak, heal, deliver, and do what only He can do.

Be Still My Soul

One of the greatest things we can do for ourselves in the Lord's presence is simply to be still. Psalm 46:10 says, "Be still, and know that I am God; I will be exalted among the nations, I will be exalted in the earth!" What treasure it is knowing we can spend our quietest moments with the One exalted in the earth. The phrase "be still" means to be "idle, quiet and alone." According to The Webster Dictionary, the word "know" means "to come to know by experience or through intimate relationship, to perceive, define or to see, to become known or to be revealed." Abiding with God in quiet stillness deepens our intimacy with the Lord. As we lean into Him, we get to know His personality, His heartbeat, His righteousness, and truly all that He is.

Unlike what many have experienced in earthly relationships, God's intimacy is pure and not skewed by the world. When you're spending time being saturated in pure Love, you come out pure. This close connection with your Maker always strengthens and imparts life.

Being still is also rest. Holy Spirit brings such comfort and peace to our entire being when we are with Him. Isaiah 30:15 says, "For thus says the Lord God, the Holy One of Israel: 'In returning and rest you shall be saved; in quietness and confidence shall be your strength." The word "saved" in this passage includes such meanings as the following: to be liberated, to be granted victory in battle, and to be delivered. In other words, when we return to the Lord's presence and rest in Him, He fights our battles and wins the victory. He restores us completely. This state of resting in the Lord with nothing missing or broken reflects what the ancient Hebrews meant when they said "shalom." Shalom, or peace, is not a mere absence of conflict. It is a wholeness that comes to us through soaking and abiding in His presence. He is the only source of true peace.

Wait upon Him

Waiting upon the Lord means to meditate on His words. To meditate on anything is to give it full focus, to fully consider or ponder. When we meditate on God's word, that's exactly what we're doing. We focus our attention on Him and position ourselves to hear and obey. What is God saying? What does He want to do? Do we move forward or stay put?

In the waiting place we find confidence and strength for our journey with God. Isaiah 40:31 says, "But those who wait on the Lord shall renew their strength; They shall mount up with wings like eagles, they shall run and not be weary, they shall walk and not faint." There is no formula for what waiting should look like. Rather, with a heart of obedience find a place you can sit or lay down. Go sit by the river, in the closet, or under a tree. You can worship with music or just simply be quiet before Him wherever you are. The key is just to BE alone with Him. He is the Lover of our souls. Hebrews 12:2 says, *"looking unto Jesus, the author and finisher of our faith, who for the joy that was set before Him endured the cross, despis-*

ing the shame, and has sat down at the right hand of the throne of God."

How do you grow in God?

Growing in the Lord is inevitable when you put your whole heart, mind, will, and emotions into Him. This takes great discipline and submission of flesh but produces maturity. No one can make you grow in God. That is something only He can do in our hearts when we choose Him. Choosing to sit at the feet of Jesus will produce the fruits of righteousness and the very nature of Christ in us. It will always be a choice to follow when He calls. It will always be a choice to decide if we set specific time aside in our 24-hour days for Him. Satan will always try to bring distractions or excuses. This happens especially when we are intentional and serious about cultivating our time in the presence of Jesus. It's important that we keep that in mind because we do not want to be deceived. Meditating on Him and His Word will keep our hearts and minds sharp and in tune with Holy Spirit. The more we abide in Him with a sincere heart and mind, the more disciplined, diligent, and mature we become.

Great reward comes out of being with Jesus, and we see this in the story of Mary and Martha from **Luke 10:38-42**:

> *"38 Now it happened as they went that He entered a certain village; and a certain woman named Martha welcomed Him into her house. 39 And she had a sister called Mary, who also sat at Jesus' feet and heard His word. 40 But Martha was distracted with much serving, and*

> *she approached Him and said, "Lord, do You not care that my sister has left me to serve alone? Therefore, tell her to help me." 41 And Jesus answered and said to her, "Martha, Martha, you are worried and troubled about many things. 42 But one thing is needed, and Mary has chosen that good part, which will not be taken away from her."*

Mary chose to sit at the feet of Jesus; she was at complete peace. Jesus let her occupy that space and stay there. Meanwhile, Martha carried on in her busyness and let distraction be her portion. What Martha was doing truly was important, but the point was for her to take time to simply be with Jesus while He was in her midst. Yet, everything else came first with the possible hope that she'd be able to do the same later. Serving is of the Lord, but when the Lord says to come rest, abide, and be with Him in intimacy, and we choose not to, often our circumstances turn out like Martha's.

His Divine Presence

Abiding with God in quiet worship is where we learn to hear how Holy Spirit speaks to us personally. It's like practicing a sport - the more we practice, the better we become. It is no different from practicing being in His presence. Holy Spirit may show us something about Jesus through personal revelation in this alone time. He may reveal things to us about what is in our own heart. He may show us plans or blueprints for things to come. He often comes with wisdom and gives us counsel on circumstances. He will continuously pour out His love upon us, and this place of intimacy is where we learn to pour our love back out upon Him. He absolutely knows what we need and when we need it.

We find our exhortation for this deep communion in Matthew 6:32, "*...For your heavenly Father knows that you need these things. But seek first the kingdom of God and His righteousness, and all these things shall be added to you. Therefore, do not worry about tomorrow, for tomorrow will worry about its own things. Sufficient for the day is its own trouble.*" There is no limit to what God can accomplish in our hearts when we willfully spend time in Him. As we seek the Lord, we are yielded to His word and Holy Spirit. We don't try to make an encounter with God happen, nor do we "try to take ourselves" in the spirit. Any attempt to control or manipulate the Holy Spirit is witchcraft, and not of the Lord. He is master, not us, and we move in His authority and power through surrender and obedience, not self-will. Nevertheless, we learn and grow in encountering Jesus by abiding in the True Vine. It always goes back to John 15.

Open your heart to Him

In our time of worship and resting in the Lord, we want to have an open heart with Him - no holding back. Resisting God, or trying to keep anything back from Him, is the same as telling Him you don't need what He has to offer. Nothing could be more inaccurate. The truth is simple: we need God. When we acknowledge the depth of our need for God and surrender to His will, He works in us what we could never do ourselves. The openness of our hearts is the key.

Matthew 5:6 says, *"Blessed are those who hunger and thirst for righteousness, for they shall be filled."*

We don't want to be filled with anything other than the Spirit of the Living God. In Him, by Him, and through Him, we find out exactly who we are and what we were made for: to have relationship with our Creator who is all things good, lovely, whole, right, and pure. He is our Lord, our Master, our Savior, our Bridegroom, and our coming King. Even though God fulfills ALL of these amazing roles, it is absolutely amazing that He cares deeply about you and me and our time together with Him. His love is truly beyond compare; our response is to open our hearts and allow Him to love us.

Meditate on Him References:

"Therefore humble yourselves under the mighty hand of God, that He may exalt you in due time, casting all your cares upon Him for he cares for you." **1 Peter 5:6-7**

"My son, give attention to my words; incline your ear to my sayings. Do not let them depart from you eyes; Keep them in the midst of your heart; For they are life to those who find them, and health to all their flesh." **Proverbs 4:20-22**

"You will keep him in perfect peace whose mind is stayed on You because he trusts in You." **Isaiah 26:3**

"If then you were raised with Christ, seek those things which are above, where Christ is, sitting

at the right hand of God. Set your mind on things above, not on things on the earth. For you died, and your life is hidden with Christ in God. When Christ who is our life appears, then you also will appear with Him in glory. Therefore put to death your members which are on the earth: fornication, uncleanness, passion, evil desire, and covetousness, which is idolatry. Because of these things the wrath of God is coming upon the sons of disobedience, in which you yourselves once walked when you lived in them. But now you yourselves are to put off all these: anger, wrath, malice, blasphemy, filthy language out of your mouth. Do not lie to one another, since you have put off the old man with his deeds, and have put on the new man who is renewed in knowledge according to the image of Him who created him, where there is neither Greek nor Jew, circumcised nor uncircumcised, barbarian, Scythian, slave nor free, but Christ is all and in all. Therefore, as the elect of God, holy and beloved, put on tender mercies, kindness, humility, meekness, longsuffering; bearing with one another, and forgiving one another, if anyone has a complaint against another; even as Christ forgave you, so you also must do. But above all these things put on love, which is the bond of perfection. And let the peace of God rule in your hearts, to which also you were called in one body; and be thankful. Let the word of Christ dwell in you richly in all wisdom, teaching and admonishing one another in psalms and hymns and spiritual songs, singing with grace in your hearts to the Lord. And whatever you do in word or deed, do all in the name of the Lord Jesus, giving thanks to God the Father through Him. Wives, submit to your own husbands, as is fitting in the Lord.

Husbands, love your wives and do not be bitter toward them. Children, obey your parents in all things, for this is well pleasing to the Lord. Fathers, do not provoke your children, lest they become discouraged. Bondservants, obey in all things your masters according to the flesh, not with eyeservice, as men-pleasers, but in sincerity of heart, fearing God. And whatever you do, do it heartily, as to the Lord and not to men, knowing that from the Lord you will receive the reward of the inheritance; for[a] you serve the Lord Christ. But he who does wrong will be repaid for what he has done, and there is no partiality." **Colossians 3**

"This Book of the Law shall not depart from your mouth, but you shall meditate in it day and night, that you may observe to do according to all that is written in it. For then you will make your way prosperous, and then you will have good success." **Joshua 1:8**

"I will meditate on Your precepts, and contemplate Your ways." **Psalm 119:15**

"My hands also I will lift up to Your commandments, which I love, and I will meditate on Your statutes." **Psalm 119:48**

"My eyes are awake through the night watches, that I may meditate on Your word." **Psalm 119:148**

"When He had been baptized, Jesus came up immediately from the water; and behold, the heavens were opened to Him, and He saw the Spirit of God descending like a dove and alight-

ing upon Him." **Matthew 3:16**

"Finally, brethren, whatever things are true, whatever things are noble, whatever things are just, whatever things are pure, whatever things are lovely, whatever things are of good report, if there is any virtue and if there is anything praiseworthy—meditate on these things." **Philippians 4:8**

"Meditate on these things; give yourself entirely to them, that your progress may be evident to all." **1 Timothy 4:15**

"All Scripture is given by inspiration of God, and is profitable for doctrine, for reproof, for correction, for instruction in righteousness..." **2 Timothy 3:16**

"For the word of God is living and powerful, and sharper than any two-edged sword, piercing even to the division of soul and spirit, and of joints and marrow, and is a discerner of the thoughts and intents of the heart." **Hebrews 4:12**

"And so we have the prophetic word confirmed, which you do well to heed as a light that shines in a dark place, until the day dawns and the morning star rises in your hearts..." **2 Peter 1:19**

"Be angry, and do not sin. Meditate within your heart on your bed, and be still. Selah." **Psalm 4:4**

"Lead me in Your truth and teach me, for You

are the God of my salvation; on You I wait all the day." **Psalm 25:5**

Prayer for Salvation

If you have not made Jesus Christ your personal Lord and Savior, and you desire this with all your heart, then please, join me in prayer:

"Heavenly Father, I choose to believe with all my heart, Your love for me. I believe that Jesus Christ is Your Son, the Son of God, and that He is God in the flesh. I believe that You sent Him to this earth to save me. Thank You. I believe He died on the cross for my sins and He was dead and buried three days, and then rose again from the dead and that He ascended to Heaven and is now seated at Your right hand and is returning again.

Father, please forgive me for all my sin and iniquity and I choose to forgive others who have sinned against me. I give You all my heart and choose to live with You forever. I believe I have been born again according to Your Word and that I have been transferred out of the kingdom of darkness and into the kingdom of light. I declare I am forgiven and healed! Now, I ask for Holy Spirit to fill me. Jesus, baptize me in Holy Spirit and fullness in order that I may know You intimately and serve You all my days.

Thank You, Lord, for loving me. Amen."

Scriptures:

John 14:6
"6 Jesus said to him, 'I am the way, the truth, and the life. No one comes to the Father except through Me.'"

Romans 10:8-13
"8 But what does it say? 'The word is near you, in your mouth and in your heart' (that is, the word of faith which we preach): 9 that if you confess with your mouth the Lord Jesus and believe in your heart that God has raised Him from the dead, you will be saved. 10 For with the heart one believes unto righteousness, and with the mouth confession is made unto salvation. 11 For the Scripture says, 'Whoever believes on Him will not be put to shame.' 12 For there is no distinction between Jew and Greek, for the same Lord over all is rich to all who call upon Him. 13 For 'whoever calls on the name of the Lord shall be saved.'"

John 3:3-8, 16-18
"3 Jesus answered and said to him, 'Most assuredly, I say to you, unless one is born again, he cannot see the kingdom of God.' 4 Nicodemus said to Him, 'How can a man be born when he is old? Can he enter a second time into his mother's womb and be born?' 5 Jesus answered, 'Most assuredly, I say to you, unless one is born of water and the Spirit, he cannot enter the kingdom of God. 6 That which is born of the flesh is flesh, and that which is born of the Spirit is spirit. 7 Do not marvel that I said

to you, "You must be born again." 8 The wind blows where it wishes, and you hear the sound of it, but cannot tell where it comes from and where it goes. So is everyone who is born of the Spirit."'

"16 For God so loved the world that He gave His only begotten Son, that whoever believes in Him should not perish but have everlasting life. 17 For God did not send His Son into the world to condemn the world, but that the world through Him might be saved. 18 'He who believes in Him is not condemned; but he who does not believe is condemned already, because he has not believed in the name of the only begotten Son of God.'"

II Corinthians 5:17
"17 Therefore, if anyone is in Christ, he is a new creation; old things have passed away; behold, all things have become new."

I Corinthians 15:3-5
"3 For I delivered to you first of all that which I also received: that Christ died for our sins according to the Scriptures, 4 and that He was buried, and that He rose again the third day according to the Scriptures, 5 and that He was seen by Cephas, then by the twelve."

II Corinthians 5:21
"21 For He made Him who knew no sin to be sin for us, that we might become the righteousness of God in Him."

Colossians 1:13-14
"13 He has delivered us from the power of dark-

ness and conveyed us into the kingdom of the Son of His love, 14 in whom we have redemption through His blood, the forgiveness of sins."

Luke 11:9-13

"9 So I say to you, ask, and it will be given to you; seek, and you will find; knock, and it will be opened to you. 10 For everyone who asks receives, and he who seeks finds, and to him who knocks it will be opened. 11 If a son asks for bread from any father among you, will he give him a stone? Or if he asks for a fish, will he give him a serpent instead of a fish? 12 Or if he asks for an egg, will he offer him a scorpion? 13 If you then, being evil, know how to give good gifts to your children, how much more will your heavenly Father give the Holy Spirit to those who ask Him!"

Acts 1:8

"8 But you shall receive power when the Holy Spirit has come upon you; and you shall be witnesses to Me in Jerusalem, and in all Judea and Samaria, and to the end of the earth."

I Timothy 3:16

"16 And without controversy great is the mystery of godliness:

*God was manifested in the flesh,
Justified in the Spirit,
Seen by angels,
Preached among the Gentiles,
Believed on in the world,
Received up in glory."*

Fresh Infilling of Holy Spirit

Acts 1:8
"8 But you shall receive power when the Holy Spirit has come upon you; and you shall be witnesses to Me in Jerusalem, and in all Judea and Samaria, and to the end of the earth."

If you have been born again and filled with Holy Spirit and you desire MORE and want to encounter the Lord's presence afresh and anew, please join me in prayer:

"Father, in the name of Jesus, I thank You for loving me and I ask according to Ephesians 1:17-19, that You would give me the spirit of wisdom and revelation in the knowledge of Him, Jesus, and the eyes of my understanding would be enlightened; that I may know what is the hope of His calling and what are the riches of the glory of His inheritance in the saints, and what is the exceeding greatness of His power toward us who believe, according to the working of His mighty power towards us who believe, according to the working of His mighty power which He worked in Christ when He raised Him from the dead and seated Him at His right hand in the heavenly places. Amen.

Father, according to Colossians 3:9-12, I ask in Jesus name, that I would be filled with the knowledge of His will in all wisdom and spiritual understanding; that I would walk worthy of the Lord, fully pleasing Him, being fruitful in every good work and increasing in the knowledge of God; strengthened with all might, according to His glorious power. Amen.

I surrender and yield my life to the fullness of Holy Spirit; His power and anointing; the spirit of wisdom and revelation; counsel and might; the spirit of the fear of the Lord and knowledge according to Isaiah 11:2, in Jesus' name. Amen."

The Garden Training Center, Inc.
The Apostolic School of Ministry

The Garden Apostolic Training Center is a place that fosters spiritual growth. The center provides training to equip believers in Jesus Christ for the work of the ministry and to be victorious and free in all areas of their lives through the supernatural empowerment of the Holy Spirit. For more information check out **thegardenstc.org**.

The Garden Gathering Church

The purpose of The Garden Gathering Church is to encourage believers in Jesus Christ: to fully embrace the love of God; to walk in freedom; to carry His presence and glory; and to be equipped and trained for the work of the ministry through worship, teachings, and impartation.

> *"It's all about Love. When you see His eyes of Love for you, nothing else matters. That's it. That's all you need to know."*
>
> *-Brandy Helton*

www.ingramcontent.com/pod-product-compliance
Lightning Source LLC
Chambersburg PA
CBHW020548080526
44583CB00013B/1048